Contents

Growing up

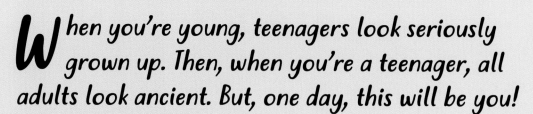

When you're young, teenagers look seriously grown up. Then, when you're a teenager, all adults look ancient. But, one day, this will be you!

At every stage of your life, your body's changing, and it has been since you were born. Sometimes, your body alters only a little, but there are times when you start to change a lot, quite quickly. One of these times is called puberty. It's when you go from being a child to being an adult, and it's what this book is all about.

During puberty, your body changes, on the outside and on the inside. You might have noticed some of these changes already, or they might not have started happening to you yet. Either way, there's nothing to worry about. Our body clocks run at different speeds, so puberty doesn't happen to everyone at the same age.

Growing up is an exciting time, but it can also feel scary, and maybe a bit embarrassing. It's not only about how your body changes, but about the way these changes affect your life, your feelings, your family and friends.

This book will help you understand more about what is happening to you, and reassure you that it is perfectly normal and natural!

What is puberty?

Puberty marks a new stage in your life. It is the time when your body grows and changes from a child's body to an adult's. These changes make it possible for you to have a baby one day, if you want to.

So, why does puberty happen? Inside your body, there are powerful chemicals, called hormones, travelling around in your blood. These hormones carry messages to different parts of your body.

You have lots of different hormones in your body. Some hormones instruct your body to grow; some control how your body uses up energy. Some get your body ready for being an adult, and that's how puberty begins.

You'll find out lots more about the changes to your body on the next pages, but here's a quick list below of what to expect. Don't worry if they don't happen in this order, or if they overlap. Everybody's body is different.

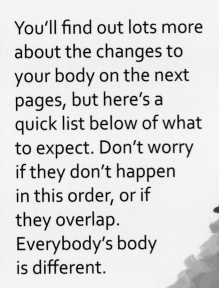

DURING PUBERTY:

- you grow taller, faster than at any other time
- your body gets curvier, and your hips get wider
- your breasts begin to grow
- your pubic hair starts growing
- hair also grows on your legs and under your arms
- you might start getting spots
- you start sweating more
- your moods keep changing
- your sex organs develop inside you
- your periods start.

When does it happen?

For most girls, puberty begins when they are about 10 or 11 years old. But it can happen at any time between the ages of 8 and 13. There's no set age for puberty to start – it depends on lots of things.

Everyone goes through puberty, but everyone develops at different times so try not to compare yourself to your friends. It doesn't matter if you start puberty earlier or later – everyone gets there in the end!

Boys go through puberty, too, usually between the ages of 11 and 15. Like girls, boys get taller and hairier, and may have to start shaving.

Their voices also 'break' and get deeper, as their voice boxes grow. While this is happening, their voices may become squeaky when they're speaking, then get deeper again. This settles down after a while, but it can make boys feel awkward.

Girls tend to go through puberty more quickly than boys. This is the reason why girls in a class are often taller than boys, and can seem older, even though they are all the same age. Girls might think that boys are a bit silly and immature, while boys might find girls quite bossy and scary. But, within a year or two, boys catch up, and things even out.

Changes outside you

The first part of this book is all about the changes that happen on the outside of your body, during puberty. They're the signs that you're likely to notice first.

One of the first clues that puberty is on its way is getting taller, quite suddenly. Between the ages of 12 and 13, you'll probably grow faster than ever before. This is called a growth spurt, and it's the reason why people keep telling you how much you've grown!

During your growth spurt, your arms and legs grow faster than the rest of your body. You might feel clumsy, and out of sorts, and find that your favourite jeans are suddenly way too short.

WHY DO MY ARMS AND LEGS ACHE?

These aches are called 'growing pains' but they don't last too long. They should go away on their own, without you needing any special treatment.

Your body will also get curvier, and your hips will get rounder. You may also put on weight. Don't worry about these changes - like everything else, they are getting your body ready for having babies, one day. And don't worry if you're more or less curvy than your friends. This also depends on your natural body shape. You're not getting fat, and you don't need to go on a diet - you are growing up! It just might take a little while to get used to your new shape.

Getting hairier

During puberty, your body starts to get hairier. You'll notice that you start to grow hair in places you didn't have hair before – around your groin, under your arms, and on your legs.

The hair that grows in a triangle around your groin is called pubic hair. It's usually the first hair to sprout. It starts off quite soft and pale, but soon gets darker and curlier. Pubic hair never grows very long, but it can be quite bushy. Some girls have quite thick pubic hair. Others have hardly any. You may also have a few hairs on your tummy.

About a year after your pubic hair grows, you'll see hair sprouting in your armpits. Hair also starts growing on your arms and legs. The hair on your top lip might get darker, too.

While all this hair sounds a bit scary, it's nothing to be alarmed about. Getting hairier is just a normal part of growing up, and it happens to everyone.

When you're older, you might want to get rid of some of it, but ask your mum or an older sister or aunt first. You need to think about it carefully. If it doesn't bother you, leave it where it is.

WHY AM I GETTING HAIRY?

Humans are related to apes, but luckily, we've got much less hair than our ancestors thousands of years ago. No one is quite sure why people grow pubic and armpit hair, though.

Growing breasts

Breasts are mainly for making milk to feed babies that you might have one day, and they're an obvious sign that your body's changing. Some girls can't wait for this to happen. Others might feel a bit self-conscious or awkward, until they get used to it.

The first thing you might notice is that your nipples stick out from your chest. Next, a small bump, called a breast bud, grows underneath. As fat fills the space behind your nipples, your breasts get bigger, while your nipples get bigger and darker. Your breasts might feel tingly or tender, but this will soon wear off.

It's easy to feel anxious if your breasts are bigger or smaller than your friends', or start growing earlier or later. But all of this is normal, and nothing to worry about. Breasts come in lots of different sizes - small, medium and large.

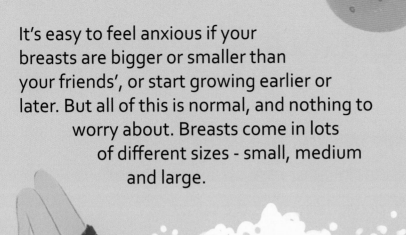

WHY IS ONE BREAST BIGGER THAN THE OTHER?

One breast may grow faster than the other to begin with, but they usually even out. That said, almost half of women have breasts of different sizes.

Wearing a bra

When your breasts start to grow larger, and feel heavier, you may decide to get a bra. You don't have to wear a bra at all, of course, but a bra will help to support your breasts so that you feel more comfortable.

Finding a bra that fits properly is really important, so it's worth taking time ove it. The bra needs to fit snugly around your chest, and the cups shouldn't be so tight that you bulge out of them, nor so loose that the material sags.

There are lots of guides to measuring yourself for a bra, or you can go to a large shop that offers a free bra-measuring service. The shop assistants will be happy to help you, but take your mum or a friend along, if you're feeling nervous.

Once you've been measured, you can choose your bra! There are lots of different styles and colours to try on. If you can't decide which ones are best, put your top on over each bra to check if it fits well, and gives you a good shape.

MY BRA SIZE IS 32 AA. WHAT DOES THIS MEAN?

The '32' is the measurement around your chest (in inches, though it can be in centimetres). The 'AA' is your cup size. Combining both gives you your bra size.

Changes inside you

You've found out about the changes that happen on the outside of your body as you go through puberty. But what about the changes on the inside? You can't see these changes taking place, but it's useful, and reassuring, to know what's happening.

During puberty, your sex organs develop and grow. They are tucked low down inside your tummy, and their job is to get your body ready for having babies.

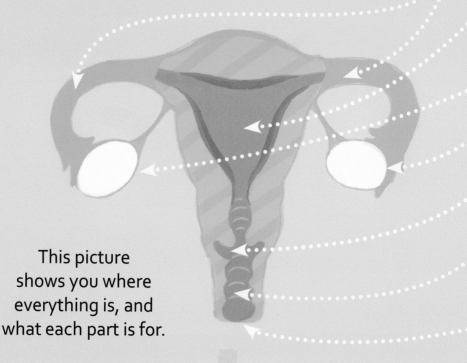

This picture shows you where everything is, and what each part is for.

FALLOPIAN TUBES

These two tubes run from your ovaries to your womb. Eggs travel along them.

WOMB (UTERUS)

This is where a baby grows, if a woman becomes pregnant. The womb stretches as the baby grows bigger.

OVARIES

Your two ovaries are where your eggs are stored. For a baby to begin, an egg from a woman must join with a sperm from a man

CERVIX

This narrow passageway connects your womb to your vagina.

VAGINA

This stretchy tube leads from the outside of your body to your womb.

VULVA

These are the sex organs on the outside of your body. They're also called genitals.

Having a period

One of the biggest changes you'll go through during puberty is starting your periods. This means that, for a few days every month, you'll get some bleeding from your vagina. This might sound scary, but don't worry - this is a completely normal and healthy part of growing up.

A period happens because, once a month, an egg from your ovaries moves down a fallopian tube towards your womb. Your womb grows a thick lining of blood vessels so that a baby could grow there. But if the egg doesn't meet a sperm and make a baby, it breaks up, along with the womb lining. The lining then comes out of your vagina as blood.

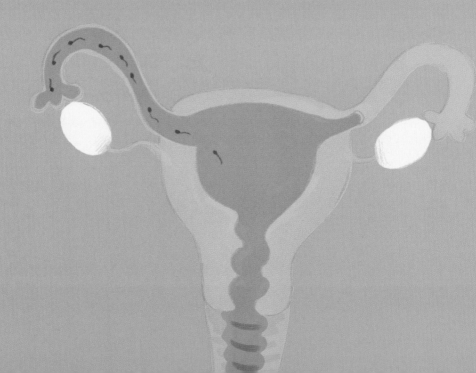

You'll probably start your periods between the ages of 11-14, but it could be earlier or later than that.

Just before your period starts, you might notice a yellow or white stain in your pants. Your breasts might feel tender, and your tummy might ache a bit. These are nothing to worry about. Once your period starts, they should clear up.

WHAT DOES 'COMING ON' MEAN?

It's just another way of saying that your period's started. Some people also call periods their 'time of the month'.

Using towels

While you're on your period, you'll need to wear something to soak up the blood. Most girls start off with sanitary towels (pads), then may try tampons (see page 24) later. You can buy towels and tampons at a supermarket or chemist's.

Towels are strips of absorbent material that you stick inside your pants. They come in different shapes and thicknesses. You might need a thicker towel at the beginning of your period, when the blood is heavier, and at night, when you wear the same towel for longer. Choose a thinner towel for other times. Try out a few different brands and types of towels to find the right ones for you.

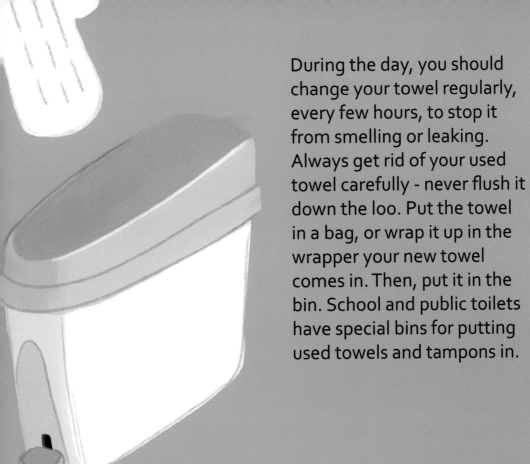

During the day, you should change your towel regularly, every few hours, to stop it from smelling or leaking. Always get rid of your used towel carefully - never flush it down the loo. Put the towel in a bag, or wrap it up in the wrapper your new towel comes in. Then, put it in the bin. School and public toilets have special bins for putting used towels and tampons in.

WHAT IF MY TOWEL SHOWS THROUGH MY CLOTHES?

The towels you can buy are so thin that no one will ever know that you're wearing one of them.

Using tampons

Tampons are little rolls of absorbent material, with a short string at the end. They fit inside your vagina, where they swell up and soak up any blood. Tampons come in different sizes. It's best to use the smallest size you need. You will need to use different sizes for heavier and lighter days.

Some girls prefer tampons because, apart from the string, you can't see or feel them when they're in place. But they can be a bit tricky to get used to at first. Like towels, you should change your tampon regularly. If you leave one in for too long, you could get toxic shock syndrome – a very rare but very serious illness.

Before putting in a tampon, make sure your hands are clean. Push the tampon into your vagina, using your finger or the applicator (a plastic or cardboard tube). Push the applicator up.

Pull all of the cardboard out and the tampon should remain comfortably in place inside you. If it feels uncomfortable, then it's probably not quite far enough in. Take it out and try again with a new tampon.

To take the tampon out, pull gently on the string. Tampons can be flushed down the loo, but it is better for the environment to wrap them up and put them in a bin. It can sometimes take several practices before you can easily insert a tampon.

Period pains

Once you get used to them, you may not have any problems with your periods. You'll learn to cope with them, and carry on with life as normal.

But you might find that, a few days before you start your period, you feel more tired and grumpy than usual. Your tummy may feel bloated, and you might get a headache or backache.

These things are all caused by the changing levels of hormones in your body during your monthly cycle. They're part of growing up, and are usually nothing to worry about.

Some girls get aches, like cramp, in their tummies. These aches are called 'period pains'. They happen when the muscles in your womb squeeze to push the blood out. They are usually mild, and wear off in a day or two, but if they are very painful, there are various things you can do. Try soaking in a hot bath or putting a hot water bottle on your tummy. Even doing some exercise can help. If these don't work, you could ask your parents for a painkiller.

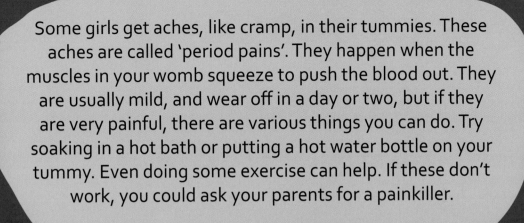

If the pain gets too bad, or lasts for longer than a few days, make sure that you tell someone. You might need to go to see the doctor.

All about periods

It's normal to feel nervous about starting your periods, and you'll probably have loads of questions. You might find some of the answers here or you can ask someone you trust.

How long will my period last?
Your period can last between 3-8 days, but it's usually around 5. The first two days often have the heaviest blood loss.

How much blood will come out?
You'll only lose a small amount of blood – around 5 to 12 teaspoons – during your period. It seeps out slowly, not all in one go.

What if I come on at school?
You can ask a teacher or the school nurse for a towel or tampon. Don't feel embarrassed – they're used to it. You could also keep a small supply in your locker or school bag.

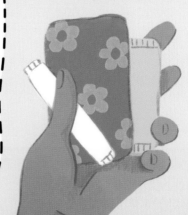

Why haven't I started yet?

Everyone grows up at different rates, so you may start later than your friends. Most girls will have regular periods by the time they're 16.

Can I still do P.E.?

Yes, you can! But, if you're going swimming, you'll need to wear a tampon. You can't go swimming in a towel.

Does it hurt to put a tampon in?

It might feel a bit odd or uncomfortable at first, but it doesn't hurt. Try to relax – that will help the tampon go in more easily.

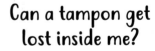

Can a tampon get lost inside me?

No, it can't. It stays in your vagina and can't go any further because the opening into your womb is too small.

When do periods stop?

Your periods will probably stop altogether in your late 40s or early 50s. But you'll have fewer periods in the months or years before then. This is called the menopause.

Looking after yourself

Everything that's happening, on the inside and outside of your body, uses up huge amounts of energy. It's no wonder you might feel tired and grumpy. To help you cope better, you'll need to look after yourself. Things like eating healthily, keeping fit and getting plenty of sleep will make a big difference.

A good night's sleep is important when you're growing up. It gives your busy body a chance to recharge. It's also the time when your body makes a hormone that helps you grow. During puberty, though, your sleep patterns may change. You might have no trouble staying up late, but not be able to wake up easily the next morning.

IF YOU'RE TIRED, BUT CAN'T GO
TO SLEEP, THERE ARE LOTS OF THINGS
YOU CAN TRY. FOR STARTERS ...

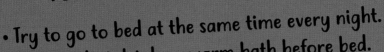

- Try to go to bed at the same time every night.
- Have a hot drink or warm bath before bed.
- Make your bedroom comfortable – not too hot or cold.
- Turn off any tech at least an hour before you go to bed.
- Try not to lie there worrying – count some sheep instead!

HOW MUCH SLEEP DO I NEED?

Between the ages of 5 and 12, you need
about 10 or 11 hours' sleep a night.
Teenagers should get around 9 hours'
sleep, but different people need more
or less sleep than that.

Healthy eating

During puberty, you'll probably feel hungry nearly all the time. This is because you're growing and changing so fast. Your body is burning up loads of energy, and needs refuelling regularly.

To cope with all the changes, and stay healthy, it's best to eat a balanced diet. This means eating a mixture of different types of food. Look at the illustration below. It shows you how much of each type of food you should eat.

Pasta, rice, bread and cereals

Fruit and vegetables

Fats

Eggs, beans, fish and meat

Milk, cheese and dairy

When hunger strikes, it's tempting to reach for something quick, like biscuits or a bag of crisps. It's fine to have sweet or fatty food as a treat, but try to stick to healthy snacks, most of the time. Fruit, plain popcorn and yoghurts are tasty, and will do just as good a job at filling you up.

The best drinks are water, semi-skimmed milk and sugar-free drinks. Fruit juice, smoothies and many fizzy drinks are packed with sugar which rots your teeth. It's okay to have them every now and then, but not every day.

DO I NEED TO GO ON A DIET?

It's normal, during puberty, to put on a bit of weight, especially on your tummy and hips. This helps your body cope with all the changes. It doesn't mean you're getting fat, and you don't need to go on a diet.

Getting moving

As well as eating healthily, it's good to keep fit and active during puberty. Exercise will help you look better, making your body stronger, and keeping your weight healthy. It will also help you feel good - you'll sleep better and feel happier and less stressed.

It's easy to make excuses not to do exercise. The trick is to find an activity you enjoy – you're more likely to stick at it that way. You don't have to be a sports' ace – just find something that gets you moving.

Not all exercise involves running, going to the gym, or getting yourself picked for a school team. Taking the dog for a walk, dancing around your room or mowing the lawn all count as exercise, too.

Here are some suggestions for other **ACTIVITIES** you could try.

- Walking
- Jogging
- Swimming
- Dancing
- Gymnastics

- Tennis
- Netball
- Horse-riding
- Scootering
- Roller-skating

- Biking
- Rock climbing
- Martial arts
- Football

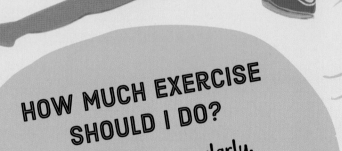

HOW MUCH EXERCISE SHOULD I DO?

Try to exercise regularly. If possible, aim for at least an hour a day, five times a week, but you can break this down into shorter chunks.

Keeping clean

You'll notice you start to sweat more as you're growing up. Don't worry - everybody sweats sometimes. Sweating helps to cool our bodies down.

If sweat mixes with bacteria on your skin, it can start to smell. This is called body odour (B.O.). To stop this, you'll need to wash more often than you did before. If you can, have a bath or shower every day, and after doing exercise.

You can also use a deodorant under your arms. Change your clothes regularly so they don't get smelly, especially your tops, socks and underwear.

If smelly armpits aren't enough, you'll probably get spots (acne) on your face, too. They're caused by oil in your skin clogging up your pores. Try not to pick at or squeeze them. It'll make them last longer, and they might get infected.

Wash your face in warm water twice a day with mild soap or cleanser. You can also buy spot treatments from the chemist. Eating a healthy diet and drinking plenty of water will help your skin to look good.

WHY IS MY HAIR SO GREASY?

This is because of the same oil that causes spots. You might need to wash your hair every day, for a while, and use a shampoo for greasy hair.

Mixed feelings

Are you happy one minute, then down in the dumps the next? Does everyone and everything drive you mad? It's not nice, but these changing moods and feelings are a normal part of growing up.

As you're discovering, your hormones cause your body to change physically, but they also play tricks with your feelings. You might find yourself getting angry, but having no idea why. You might end up falling out with your friends, for no reason, or just wishing that everyone would leave you alone. It's confusing and scary, but, in time, your hormones, and feelings, will settle down again.

It takes a while to get used to your new self during puberty, and you might feel more self-conscious. You might think people are looking at you, or that nobody likes you. Most likely, neither of these things are true, but they can feel very real, and hurtful, at the time. It's important to be proud of the new you, both inside and out.

WHY DO I GET SO ANGRY?

Everyone gets angry. It's how you handle it that's important, so learn ways of staying in control. One way is to force yourself to count to 10 (or more) until you feel calmer again.

Friends and family

Everyone falls out with their friends and family sometimes. But, during puberty, you might find this happens more often.

Some friendships can last for years. But friendships may change during puberty, as you and your friends grow up at different rates, and get interested in different things. You might make new friends, and lose touch with old ones. Your best friends may change from week to week, then change back again!

Things can also get tricky with your parents. You're keen to be an adult, but think your parents are still treating you like a child. You might have a big row, and tell them you hate them (you don't really). Try to remember that your parents are just trying to keep you safe and happy.

Puberty's also the time when you might start fancying boys. This can feel exciting, but scary at the same time. You might have a crush on a boy, and get a funny feeling inside when you see him. You desperately want him to notice you, but, if he does, you want to run away and hide. Not all girls fancy boys – some fancy other girls.

Amazing you!

So, now you've found out lots about puberty and, hopefully, you feel more confident about what's happening to you. One thing's for certain - puberty is like riding a rollercoaster, with lots of ups and down.

By the end of puberty, you might have grown taller than your mum (and maybe your dad). You'll have developed breasts and started your periods. You'll have fallen out with your friends, made up and fallen out again. You'll probably have had a serious crush on someone, and you'll definitely have been driven mad by almost everyone. It's exciting, but exhausting, so make sure that you've read the pages on getting a good night's sleep.

Everyone goes through puberty, and everyone has good times, and not-such-good times, as they experience all the amazing changes. Knowing more about what's happening will help you get used to how things are changing.

If you do get worried about anything, remember, you're not on your own and you don't have to bottle things up. There are always people you can talk to and go to for help. If it's difficult talking to your parents, try a favourite teacher, learning mentor, school nurse, or a friend's parents. You'll also find lots more information and advice on the next two pages.

Good Luck!

Further advice

We hope that you have found this book useful, and that will help you to understand what puberty is all about. It's important to remember that puberty is a natural and normal part of growing up. If you are worried about anything, though, try talking to your friends. You'll probably find that they're worrying about exactly the same things as you! You could also talk to a trusted adult, such as a parent or carer, teacher, aunt or older sister.

If you don't feel that you can talk to the people around you, there are lots of places that offer advice and help. Here are just a few ...

Websites

www.childline.org.uk
The ChildLine website offers lots of advice and information about all aspects of puberty and growing up. They also run a 24-hour helpline for young people who are having problems.

www.nhs.uk/live-well
This National Health Service website has information about puberty for girls and boys, and videos of teenagers talking about growing up and the ways that they are coping.

www.becomingateen.co.uk
A website from Lil-lets, a company who make tampons. It covers everything teenagers need to know about puberty, periods and how to choose the best sanitary products to use.

www.healthforteens.co.uk
This website has been produced by school nurses, in consultation with young people. It gives advice about how to stay healthy, both physically and mentally, during puberty.

Further reading

Healthy for Life series: *Food and Eating/Keeping Fit/Self-esteem and Mental Health* by Anna Claybourne (Franklin Watts, 2018)

It's My Body! A Book about Body Privacy by Louise Spilsbury (Franklin Watts, 2018)

Positively Teenage: a positively brilliant guide to teenage well-being by Nicola Morgan (Franklin Watts, 2018)

Puberty in Numbers: Everything You Need to Know about Growing Up by Liz Flavell (Franklin Watts, 2019)

The Girl Files: All About Puberty and Growing Up (Wayland, 2012)

Glossary

Absorbent Made from a material that soaks up liquid easily

Acne Red spots on the skin that often appear during puberty

Applicator A tube made from plastic or cardboard that you can use to push a tampon inside

Bacteria Tiny living things that can be helpful or harmful

Bloated Feeling swollen and uncomfortable

Body odour A smell caused by sweat mixing with bacteria on your skin. Also called B.O

Cramp A sharp, squeezing pain in the tummy

Crush Fancying someone very strongly, even if they don't fancy you back

Cups The cup-shaped parts of a bra that cover your breasts

Fancying Finding another boy or girl very attractive

Groin The part of your body where your legs join your abdomen (trunk)

Growing pains Aches and pains that you might feel as your body grows during puberty

Growth spurt When you get taller over a short period of time during puberty

Hormones Strong chemicals that travel around your body in your blood. They carry messages to different parts of your body, affecting what they do.

Immature Appearing younger than you are; not very grown up

Menopause When a woman's ovaries stop making eggs, and her periods stop

Periods A few days of bleeding from your vagina that happens every month

Pore Tiny opening in the skin

Pubic hair Short, wiry hair that grows around your sex organs on the outside of your body

Sanitary towel Strip of absorbent material that sticks in your pants and soaks up blood during your period

Sex organs The parts of your body that are used to make babies

Tampon Small roll of absorbent material that you put inside your vagina to soak up blood during your period

Index